6/2/88

D1288437

COVER: **'THE POSTMAN'**

THE POSTMAN, MR. ROULIN, IS MADE OF LINES THAT SWIRL AND CURL IN A WHIRLPOOL OF COLORS. IT IS A DETAILED PORTRAIT OF A ROBUST MAN, PROUD OF HIS WORK.

VINCENT VAN GOGH PERHAPS IS SHOWING US WITH THE GREEN BACKGROUND THAT THIS MAN'S WORK SURROUNDS HIM WITH GRASS, FLOWERS, SUNLIGHT AND FRESH AIR. WE SEE THAT THE WELL-GROOMED POSTMAN HAS A CURLED BEARD AS CAREFULLY TENDED AS THE TIED BLOSSOMS BEHIND HIM.

KRULLER-MULLER FOUNDATION, OTTERLO

THE ROAD TO TARASCON                    KUNSTHAUS, ZURICH

PORTRAIT OF CAMILLE ROULIN                    COLLECTION OF MR. AND MRS. RODOLPHE MEYER DE SCHAUENSEE, DEVON, PENNSYLVANIA

DEDICATED TO MILDRED AND JOE RABOFF AND THEIR CHILDREN,

MY COUSINS, PAUL RABOFF AND FLORA GOLDEN

LIBRARY OF CONGRESS CATALOGING-IN-PUBLICATION DATA
RABOFF, ERNEST LLOYD.
   VINCENT VAN GOGH.
   (ART FOR CHILDREN)
REPRINT. ORIGINALLY PUBLISHED: GARDEN CITY, N.Y.: DOUBLEDAY, 1973. SUMMARY: A BRIEF BIOGRAPHY OF VINCENT VAN GOGH ACCOMPANIES FIFTEEN COLOR REPRODUCTIONS AND CRITICAL INTERPRETATIONS OF HIS WORKS. 1. GOGH, VINCENT VAN, 1853-1890 — JUVENILE LITERATURE. 2. PAINTERS — NETHERLANDS — BIOGRAPHY — JUVENILE LITERATURE. 3. PAINTING, DUTCH — JUVENILE LITERATURE. 4. PAINTING, MODERN — 19TH CENTURY — NETHERLANDS — JUVENILE LITERATURE. [1. GOGH, VINCENT VAN, 1853-1890. 2. ARTISTS. 3. PAINTING, DUTCH. 4. PAINTING, MODERN — 19TH CENTURY — NETHERLANDS] I. TITLE. II. SERIES. ND653.G7R25 1988 759.9492 [92] 87-45315 ISBN 0-397-32230-5

# VINCENT VAN GOGH

By Ernest Raboff

# ART
# FOR
# CHILDREN

J. B. LIPPINCOTT · NEW YORK

# VINCENT VAN GOGH WAS BORN

ON MARCH 30, 1853 AT GROOTZUNDERT, HOLLAND. HIS FATHER, THEODORUS, WAS A PREACHER. ANNA CORNELIA, HIS MOTHER, CAME FROM A FAMILY OF BOOKBINDERS. VINCENT AND HIS BROTHER THEO HAD THREE SISTERS.

FROM THE AGE OF SIXTEEN TO TWENTY-THREE, YOUNG VAN GOGH WORKED IN HIS UNCLE'S ART GALLERIES IN HOLLAND, ENGLAND AND FRANCE AND MASTERED THE THREE LANGUAGES. HE ALSO STUDIED THE MANY ART MASTERPIECES IN THOSE CITIES.

FOUR YEARS LATER, AFTER STUDYING FOR THE MINISTRY AND SERVING BRIEFLY AS A PREACHER, HE DEDICATED HIS LIFE TO PAINTING AND DRAWING. AMONG HIS MANY ARTIST FRIENDS WERE EMILE BERNARD, PAUL GAUGUIN, GEORGES SEURAT, CAMILLE PISSARRO AND HENRI ROUSSEAU. IN THE FINAL TEN YEARS OF HIS LIFE HE CREATED OVER ONE THOUSAND SEVEN HUNDRED WORKS OF ART.

HE DEVELOPED A GENIUS FOR USING COLOR. THIS FRESH VISION OPENED A NEW WORLD FOR LATER ARTISTS TO EXPLORE.
AT AGE 37, VINCENT DIED. IN ADDITION TO HIS ART, HE LEFT A RICH PHILOSOPHY OF LIFE IN HIS LETTERS TO THEO.

PORTRAIT OF THE ARTIST BY ERNEST RABOFF

# VINCENT VAN GOGH WROTE:

"IT IS BETTER TO LIVE THAN WORK AT ART...HOME COMES FIRST AND PAINTING AFTER." "TO PAINT NATURE ONE MUST LIVE IN IT A LONG TIME." "PEOPLE WILL UNDERSTAND THE CURIOUS RELATIONS WHICH EXIST BETWEEN ONE FRAGMENT OF NATURE AND ANOTHER, WHICH EXPLAIN EACH OTHER."

"THERE IS NOTHING IN THE WORLD AS INTERESTING AS PEOPLE...ONE CAN NEVER STUDY THEM ENOUGH."

"IF ONE IS MASTER OF ONE THING AND UNDERSTANDS ONE THING WELL, ONE HAS AT THE SAME TIME INSIGHT INTO AND UNDERSTANDING OF MANY THINGS."

"IT IS GOOD TO LOVE MANY THINGS, FOR THEREIN LIES STRENGTH, AND WHOSOEVER LOVES MUCH PERFORMS MUCH, AND CAN ACCOMPLISH MUCH, AND WHAT IS DONE WITH LOVE IS WELL DONE."

"EVERYTHING THAT IS REALLY GOOD AND BEAUTIFUL, OF INWARD MORAL, SPIRITUAL AND SUBLIME BEAUTY IN HUMAN BEINGS AND IN THEIR WORKS COMES FROM GOD."

"THE HARVEST" IS AN EXCELLENT
EXAMPLE OF VINCENT VAN GOGH'S
METHOD OF PAINTING TO TELL A STORY.

HE USES TEXTURES, FORMS AND
COLORS LIKE A WRITER USES WORDS.
IN THIS PAINTING, FIELDS OF WHEAT,
SLIM FENCES, HAYSTACK, LADDER,
CARTS, A WOMAN IN HER GARDEN,
WORKING FARMERS AND THEIR BARNS ARE ARRANGED FOR US TO
READ LIKE SENTENCES. IN THE CENTER OF THE PICTURE, THE
TROTTING HORSE PULLING ITS PASSENGERS LEADS OUR ATTENTION
TO THE FARMER PITCHING HAY INTO HIS TALL BARN LOFT.
WITH BRIGHT STROKES OF RED, VAN GOGH ENLIVENS THE NEAT
FIELDS AND ROOFS FOR THE COUPLE WALKING DOWN THE DISTANT ROAD.

BEYOND GREEN AND BLUE HEDGE FENCES, WE NOTICE THE PALE
RANGE OF HILLS AND THE OUTLINES OF A FRENCH VILLAGE.

CONCLUDING THE PICTURE-STORY IS A WIDE EXPANSE OF CLEAR
BLUE SKY.

THE SOWER          STEDELIJK MUSEUM, AMSTERDAM

VAN GOGH
WROTE:
"I WANT TO
PAINT
SOMETHING
ETERNAL
WHICH
WE SEEK TO
GIVE BY THE
VIBRATIONS
OF OUR
COLORING."

LANDSCAPE WITH WINDMILL          GEMEENTE MUSEUM, AMSTERDAM

THE HARVEST                                    STEDELIJK MUSEUM, AMSTERDAM

"DAISES AND ANEMONES" IS A PAINTING OF CAREFULLY ORCHESTRATED COLORS. IT IS MUSIC FOR THE EYES.

VINCENT VAN GOGH LOVED MUSIC AND KNEW THAT COLORS VIBRATE MAKING VISUAL MELODIES LIKE NOTES PLUCKED ON GUITAR STRINGS.

EACH BRIGHT BLOSSOM AND EVERY PETAL AND POLLENED STALK SEND OFF SHIMMERING WAVES OF LIGHT.

RED AND WHITE TRUMPET THEIR COLOR NOTES UPWARD WHILE THE BLUES, YELLOWS AND THE ORANGES ARE ARRANGED BELOW.

AT THE RIGHT, A SINGLE PURPLE FLOWER STANDS OUT LIKE A SOLO BEAT.

VAN GOGH WROTE: "MY BRUSH GOES BETWEEN MY FINGERS AS A BOW ON A VIOLIN."

GARDEN ENTRANCE

GEMEENTE MUSEUM, AMSTERDAM

DAISES AND ANEMONES

"VINCENT'S BEDROOM AT ARLES" IS A VERY NEAT ROOM. THE ARTIST'S BLUE JACKETS AND BROWN HAT ARE HUNG ON A ROW OF PEGS BEHIND HIS STURDY, WELL-MADE BED. IT LOOKS INVITING WITH ITS WARM RED BLANKET. THE BLUE BASIN AND PITCHER, THE WATER GLASS, BOTTLE AND THE TOILET ARTICLES HAVE BEEN ARRANGED WITH THOUGHT AND REASON. WHITE AND RED TOWELS HANG FROM A LONG NAIL. FINALLY, THERE ARE TWO CHAIRS, ONE AT THE HEAD OF THE BED, THE OTHER NEAR THE DOOR.

VAN GOGH'S USE OF BLUE GIVES THE ROOM A SENSE OF SPACE, PEACE AND QUIET. THE LINES OF THE FLOOR SEEM TO ADD TO ITS LENGTH. THE TALL SHUTTERED WINDOW GIVES A FEELING OF HEIGHT.

THE ARTIST WROTE TO HIS BROTHER, THEO: "HERE COLOR IS TO DO EVERYTHING... SUGGESTIVE OF REST OR SLEEP. LOOKING AT THE PICTURE OUGHT TO REST THE BRAIN OR RATHER THE IMAGINATION ..THE BROAD LINES OF THE FURNITURE AGAIN MUST EXPRESS... REST."

VINCENT'S HOUSE AT ARLES                    VINCENT VAN GOGH MUSEUM, AMSTERDAM

VINCENT'S BEDROOM AT ARLES

DISH, KNIVES & KETTLE    VAN GOGH MUSEUM, AMSTERDAM

"GAUGUIN'S ARMCHAIR" IS A BRIGHT, FRIENDLY SCENE IN GREEN, YELLOW, RED AND BLUE. THE RICHLY COLORED WALL LOOKS LIKE A GREEN CHALKBOARD THAT IS WAITING TO BE USED.

THE CHAIR'S ARMS SEEM TO BE REACHING OUT TO WELCOME US. THE GREEN AND YELLOW-LINED SEAT LOOKS AS THOUGH IT WOULD BE VERY COMFORTABLE TO SIT ON. ALTHOUGH WE DO NOT SEE GAUGUIN IN THE PICTURE, WE FEEL HIS PRESENCE NEARBY BECAUSE OF THE TWO CANDLES STILL BURNING IN THEIR HOLDERS AND HIS BOOKS RESTING ON THE SEAT OF HIS CHAIR.

THE VIBRANT GREEN AND YELLOW COLORS BLEND UNDER THE CANDLE LIGHT TO CAST BLUE SHADOWS ON THE LEGS AND THE RUNGS OF THE CHAIR.

THESE COLORS AND THE CURVING LINES OF THE WOOD GIVE VAN GOGH'S PAINTING OF THE CHAIR DIGNITY, PERSONALITY AND CHARACTER. THE CHAIR ALMOST SEEMS READY TO SPEAK.

THE ARTIST ADDS STILL MORE FEELING OF LIFE TO THIS EXCITING PORTRAIT WITH THE GLOWING REDS, ORANGES AND YELLOWS OF THE RUG. THE COLORS ARE SCATTERED LIKE FLOWERS IN A FIELD. WE ARE REMINDED OF HOW CLOSELY HE LIVED, STUDIED AND WORKED WITH HIS GREAT FRIEND AND FELLOW ARTIST, PAUL GAUGUIN.

BOWL, DISH & SPOON    VAN GOGH MUSEUM, AMSTERDAM

GAUGUIN'S ARMCHAIR

STUDY OF 8 HANDS    VAN GOGH MUSEUM, AMSTERDAM

THE ZOUAVE    GUGGENHEIM MUSEUM, NEW YORK
THANNHAUSER COLLECTION

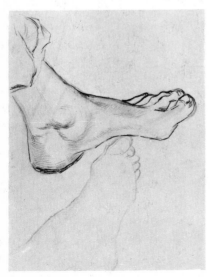

STUDY OF FEET, VAN GOGH MUSEUM, AMSTERDAM

"THE ZOUAVE" (ZOO-AH´-VAY)

IS A PAINTING OF A FRENCH SOLDIER FROM NORTH AFRICA.
THESE WERE SIMPLE, HARDY MEN.

VAN GOGH POSED THE SOLDIER IN A SETTING THAT WOULD DRAW OUR ATTENTION TO HIS RUGGED HEAD WITH ITS TASSELED HAT AND TO HIS DARKLY TANNED AND TOUGH-LOOKING HANDS.

HE IS FRAMED BY THE PALE WALL, THE GREEN BENCH AND CURTAIN AND BY THE BRICK-TILED FLOOR.
THE ZOUAVE'S SASHED BLUE AND BRIGHT RED COSTUME, TENTING OUT ABOVE HIS WHITE LEGGINGS AND BLACK BOOTS, EXCITES OUR SENSES WITH COLOR.

THE SOLDIER'S BODY SEEMS
RELAXED
BUT VAN GOGH HAS PAINTED HIM IN A POSITION OF
READINESS.
HIS INTERESTING DARK EYES
STUDY US
AND HIS HANDS SEEM TO BE
POISED FOR ACTION.

THE ZOUAVE

"PEAR TREE IN BLOSSOM" HAS THE SIMPLICITY OF A JAPANESE PRINT BY HOKUSAI, THE ORIENTAL MASTER.

VINCENT WROTE," ALL MY WORK IN A WAY IS FOUNDED ON JAPANESE ART... THEIR WORK IS AS SIMPLE AS BREATHING."

THIS PEAR TREE SEEMS ALMOST ANIMATED. IT HOLDS OUT EACH BLOSSOMING FLOWER WITH PRIDE. THE TRUNK AND BRANCHES CURVE

THE OWL, VAN GOGH MUSEUM, AMSTERDAM

GRACEFULLY LIKE THE BODY AND ARMS OF A DANCER.

BEHIND IT, THE REED FENCE, FRUIT TREES, RED BUILDING, BRICK WALL, TALL GREEN CYPRESSES AND DEEP BLUE SKY MAKE A LOVELY SETTING FOR THE

DANCE OF THE PEAR TREE.

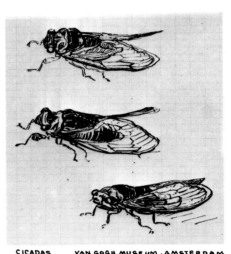

CICADAS    VAN GOGH MUSEUM, AMSTERDAM

"IT IS LOOKING AT THINGS FOR A LONG TIME THAT RIPENS AND GIVES YOU A DEEPER UNDERSTANDING", VAN GOGH ONCE WROTE.

"IF WE LOOK AT JAPANESE ART, WE SEE AN ARTIST WHO IS WISE, PHILOSOPHIC AND INTELLIGENT...THESE JAPANESE LIVE IN NATURE AS THOUGH THEY THEMSELVES WERE FLOWERS."

FOUR FLYING SWALLOWS , VAN GOGH MUSEUM, AMSTERDAM

VINCENT VAN GOGH LEARNED PAINTING WELL FROM THE JAPANESE ARTISTS WHOM HE ADMIRED.

PEAR TREE IN BLOSSOM

"THE LANGLOIS BRIDGE WITH WOMEN WASHING" IS ANOTHER EXAMPLE OF VAN GOGH'S ORIENTAL STYLE OF PAINTING. VINCENT WROTE, "YOU CANNOT STUDY JAPANESE ART WITHOUT BECOMING GAYER AND HAPPIER."

THE LANGLOIS BRIDGE AT ARLES, STAATSGALERIE, STUTTGART

SEE HOW SIMPLY HE HAS PAINTED THE LINES OF THE DRAWBRIDGE.

ABOVE THE STRUCTURE, THE CLEAR BLUE SKY CONTRASTS WITH ITS RIPPLED REFLECTION IN THE RIVER. THE YELLOW BEAMS OF THE BRIDGE MAKE A VERY INTERESTING FRAME FOR THE HORSE-DRAWN CART AND ITS DRIVER.

ALONG THE BRILLIANTLY SUNLIT SHORE PEASANT WOMEN SCRUBBING THEIR CLOTHES SEND OUT CONTINUOUS PATTERNS ACROSS THE STREAM. SLENDER REEDS OF GRASS RISE AGAINST THE RIPPLES TOWARD SIX BAMBOO-LIKE TREES.

IN A WAY, EACH OF US IS AN ARTIST.

WE SHOULD TRY TO PAINT A HAPPY STORY ON THE CANVAS OF OUR LIVES.

THE BRIDGE AT LANGLOIS, 1888   LOS ANGELES COUNTY ART MUSEUM
COLLECTION OF MR. & MRS. GEORGE GARD DE SYLVA

WOMAN AT TABLE & WOMAN STANDING
VAN GOGH MUSEUM, AMSTERDAM

LANGLOIS BRIDGE WITH WOMEN WASHING                KROLLER-MULLER FOUNDATION, OTTERLO

BRANCHES OF A PERIWINKLE
VINCENT VAN GOGH MUSEUM, AMSTERDAM

# "LA BERCEUSE" (MADAME ROULIN)

OF ARLES WAS THE WIFE OF THE POSTMAN. THE ENTIRE FAMILY, MOTHER, FATHER AND THEIR THREE CHILDREN, SAT AS MODELS FOR VINCENT VAN GOGH'S BRUSH.

VAN GOGH PAINTED MADAME AUGUSTINE ROULIN FIVE TIMES. AFTER THE THIRD, HE WROTE IN A LETTER, "I HAVE DONE 'LA BERCEUSE' THREE TIMES AND AS MRS. ROULIN WAS THE MODEL AND I ONLY THE PAINTER, I LET HER CHOOSE BETWEEN THE THREE, HER AND HER HUSBAND, BUT ON CONDITION THAT I SHOULD MAKE ANOTHER DUPLICATE FOR MYSELF OF THE ONE SHE CHOSE AND I AM WORKING ON IT NOW."

THREE WEEKS LATER HE ADDED, "SHE HAD A GOOD EYE AND CHOSE THE BEST ONE."

BRANCHES OF A FEATHER HYACINTH
VINCENT VAN GOGH MUSEUM, AMSTERDAM

VINCENT VAN GOGH WAS A THOUGHTFUL MAN AND A VERY GENEROUS ARTIST.

HE OFFERED PAUL GAUGUIN AND EMILE BERNARD, FELLOW ARTISTS, PORTRAITS OF

## MRS. AUGUSTINE ROULIN

AS A

'TOKEN OF FRIENDSHIP.'

LA BERCEUSE                                    MUSEUM OF FINE ARTS, BOSTON, BEQUEST OF JOHN T. SPAULDING

CHESTNUT LEAF AND HUSK, VAN GOGH MUSEUM, AMSTERDAM

"FRITILLARIES IN A COPPER VASE" IS AN INTERESTING PICTURE TO STUDY. THESE LILIES PAINTED BY VAN GOGH SEEM CHARGED WITH ELECTRICITY AND MAGNETISM.

ON THE TABLE, REFLECTED COLORS FROM THE BLOSSOMS, STEMS AND LEAVES STREAK INWARD TOWARD THE COPPER VASE AS THOUGH DRAWN TO A POWERFUL MAGNET.

PURPLE-BLUE STEMS AND GOLDEN FLOWERS SHOWER UP AND OUT, PEAKING AND FALLING LIKE BRIGHT COMETS, SPINNING OUR EYES AROUND THE PAINTING. THE SHIMMERING BACKGROUND IS LIKE A SKY FULL OF TINY STARS.

THE LONGER WE LOOK AT THE PAINTING THE MORE AWARE WE BECOME OF THE ELECTRICITY IT GENERATES.

WE ARE MAGNETICALLY ATTRACTED TO IT AS WE ARE TO THE SUN.

VAN GOGH WROTE, "PAINTERS UNDERSTAND NATURE AND LOVE HER AND TEACH US TO SEE HER. IF ONE REALLY LOVES NATURE ONE CAN FIND BEAUTY EVERYWHERE."

FRUIT TREE & TWO PEOPLE WORKING, VAN GOGH MUSEUM, AMSTERDAM

FRITILLARIES IN A COPPER VASE

THIS "STILL LIFE OF ORANGES AND LEMONS WITH BLUE GLOVES" HAS A WOVEN REED BASKET FILLED WITH FRUIT AND IS SURROUNDED BY GREEN SPRIGS AND BLUE GARDENING GLOVES.

IT RECALLS THE JUST COMPLETED TASK OF CUTTING AND OF PLUCKING THE TWIGS AND FRUIT. THE YELLOW AND ORANGE HARVEST AND THE ORANGE AND BLUE TINGED BRANCHES GLOW WITH THE REFLECTED COLORS OF THE ORCHARD.

WE CAN IMAGINE SOMEONE WALKING AMONG THE TREES ON A WARM, SUNNY DAY WITH A BASKET IN HAND SEARCHING OUT THE RIPE FRUIT TO PLUCK FROM THE STEMS.

WITH THE TASK FINISHED, THE GLOVES LIE ON THE TABLE LIKE A PAIR OF TIRED HANDS.

VINCENT VAN GOGH HAS PAINTED A CHEERFUL AND THOUGHTFUL WORK OF ART.

FIGURE SKETCHES            PRIVATE COLLECTOR, NEW YORK

STILL LIFE OF ORANGES AND LEMONS WITH BLUE GLOVES

COLLECTION OF MR. AND MRS. PAUL MELLON

# "THE STARRY NIGHT" EXPLODES

OUR IMAGINATIONS. WHILE THE **VILLAGE SLEEPS** IT SEEMS GUARDED BY THE POINTED CHURCH **STEEPLE** AND THE TOWERING **CYPRESS** TREE.

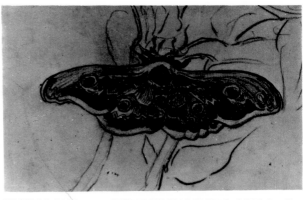

EMPEROR MOTH     VINCENT VAN GOGH MUSEUM, AMSTERDAM

**THE NIGHT SKY VIBRATES**, SWIRLS AND ROLLS IN THE STARRY HEAVEN LIKE WAVES IN A STORMY SEA. CRADLING THE TOWN PROTECTIVELY, THE HILLS SPREAD LIKE **A BLUE BLANKET OF COLOR** THEY ARE SILHOUETTED AGAINST A STRIP OF WHITE SKY REFLECTED FROM THE GOLDEN CRESCENT MOON ABOVE THEM.

**VAN GOGH** SHOWS US THE DISTANT **STARS** ORBITING IN **SPACE**. HE USES HIS BRUSH STROKES TO MAKE ELECTRIC WAVES FROM THE STARS LIKE PEBBLES DROPPED IN **WATER**.

VINCENT KNEW THAT THE **EARTH** AND **SKY**, THE **STARS** AND **TREES**, ALL THAT WE CAN SEE, ARE ALIVE. THEY ARE A PART OF **US** AND WE ARE A PART OF **THEM**.

CYPRESSES     THE BROOKLYN MUSEUM

THE STARRY NIGHT

IN THIS "PORTRAIT OF DR. GACHET," VINCENT VAN GOGH USED THREE VIBRANT HUES OF BLUE TO SURROUND THE DOCTOR'S THOUGHTFUL AND EXPRESSIVE FACE.

THE BRIGHT RED OF THE TABLE AND THE DEEP GREEN OF THE LEAVES PLACED UPON IT ARE BOLD ADDITIONS TO THE RICH BLUES.

THE DOCTOR'S LINED FACE APPEARS TO BE TIRED AND CAREWORN AGAINST THE BRILLIANT BACKGROUND. HIS EYES GAZE OUT FROM THE PORTRAIT THOUGHTFULLY.

HE SITS WITH ONE STRONG HAND RESTING ON THE TABLE'S EDGE, WHILE THE OTHER ONE SUPPORTS HIS WEARY HEAD.

WE KNOW THAT THE DOCTOR CARED FOR PEOPLE. HE WORKED DAY OR NIGHT TO MEND HIS PATIENTS, WHEREVER HE WAS NEEDED.

THIS WAS DOCTOR GACHET'S ART.

MISS GACHET AT THE PIANO     VAN GOGH MUSEUM, AMSTERDAM

PORTRAIT OF DOCTOR GACHET

ALONG THE CANAL